The Cottage Door

Cottage door

He poured forth the praises of his goods.

THE COTTAGE DOOR;

AND

What I Saw and Heard There.

London:

THE RELIGIOUS TRACT SOCIETY,

56, PATERNOSTER ROW; 65, ST. PAUL'S CHURCHYARD;
AND 164, PICCADILLY.

CONTENTS.

THE COTTAGE DOOR.

CHAPTER I.

The Ploughman.

"Oh, this old world might be better,
If each one would break a fetter."

ONE may see and hear a good many things from one's cottage door. Not that I mean to advocate for a moment the desire to "hear and to tell some new thing," which makes many a foolish person hang lazily there, to the neglect of order and comfort within. But after a long illness, and a long time of slowly getting well, being ordered to sit out in the open air, my dear mother used to place an easy chair for me under the little verandah before our cottage door; and there, while she could go in and out, or speak a cheerful word from the parlour window, I have sat many an hour, enjoying the summer air and pleasant sunshine, knitting many a stocking for poor villagers, and doing many a yard of sewing, besides reading good, useful books. And there I have made a few sketches of some I knew.

Our cottage stood on a gentle height, with a garden before it sloping down to the road, so that I needed not to suffer much intrusion from passers-by, unless I showed an inclination for their company.

In such a village as ours everybody knows everybody else, and perhaps more of one's affairs than one really knows oneself; but my mother had so resolutely set her face against village gossip, that we were happily spared the repetition of idle tales that could do no good to know. One consequence was that, when there was any matter worthy of real interest afloat, any one needing a friend, any one wanting advice, any one in trouble, we were the first to hear of it: and my mother's head and heart and hands were speedily in requisition.

I have never forgotten what she said to me one day, after a meddling visitor had talked a good deal of nonsense, in which, perhaps, I had seemed to take more than usual interest. "Ruth, dear," she said, as she tenderly smoothed the hair under my garden cap, after a brisk breeze, "I dare say you often feel lonely, and glad of a little change, and I'm always anxious you should have any that is good; but that poor thing is like a rattle, good for nothing but to make a noise; and her words should be as easily forgotten as the dried peas that make the sound. I trust that sitting here so much will not make you like gossip, Ruth."

"I trust not, dear mother; and I wish I had checked that silly, useless talk sooner."

"Well, you did the best you could when you thought about it. Dead silence is a capital way. It is often the ha, and the hum, and the yes, and no, of the listener, that plays battledore to the gossip's shuttle-cock; but drop the bat, and the game ends.

If we can do any good let us never hesitate to hear and to speak; for there is a 'time to speak' as well as a time to be silent; and, as I read lately, 'opportunity is the flower of time: use it therefore ere it withers.'"

I liked the thought, and loved the dear voice that spoke it; and when one turns one's mind into a profitable channel, it is remarkable how soon one finds "opportunity" to cultivate. Next to our garden, and running down one side of it, was a large field, where many a good crop had grown, and which was again under preparation. A plough and fine horses, followed by a labourer, appeared on the scene; and it was wonderful how the creatures seemed to understand their work, and walked up and down in straight lines, as if they knew something of geometry, and meant to make a model field of it. But I soon found that the ploughman was not of my opinion, for he scolded and grumbled and swore at the animals in the most awful manner; and at last, disgusted and sick at heart with such frightful interruption to the sweet harmonies of nature, I retired within doors.

"It is indeed bad for the listener; but think what it is for the speaker, Ruth," said my mother. "What must be the state of the heart from which proceed such blasphemy and foolishness?"

That evening my mother spent an hour in finding out who the man was, where he lived, and what the condition of his family. "It was of no use to complain and remonstrate merely," she said; "we must take an interest in him and his, and try to overcome evil with good." Doubtless she saw "opportunity," and the flower should not wither at her feet. She called to see Jacob Grindle's wife, and found a busy, slatternly, grumbling woman, who seemed to have lost heart in all human things, without finding a place in it for higher and holier things. Six or seven children scrambled about; and now and then a muttered oath might be heard amidst the group when they gathered together. My mother soon made friends with the children, then with their mother; and several little comforts found their way into the cottage, which made it seem worth while to clean up and be tidy, notwithstanding that Jacob would give her no thanks for the trouble, but stay and drink at the nearest public-house until his money was gone; and then there was nothing but oaths and anger left for his hapless home.

"Now, Ruth, dear," said my mother, "pray for me. I am going to speak to Jacob himself to-night, in the name of the Lord whom he is constantly blaspheming."

I knew that she had been praying for herself and for him, and the sweet look of peace and decision on her face seemed to me an earnest of success. Ah! reader, would you be truly a worker for God, would you do lasting good to a fellow-creature? then go straight from your knees, go in the spirit of prayer, and so shall you go in "the strength of the Lord and in the power of His might."

Jacob had been in the field all the afternoon, and had sworn alike at plough and horses, stones, clods, and weeds, and had cursed them and himself by turns. The children were in bed, Jacob was smoking a pipe, and his wife was trying some knitting which my mother had set for her.

My mother looked carefully round her and sat down. "I am very glad to see you safe at home, Mr. Grindle," said she.

"Thank ye, ma'am; don't know what should hinder it," said he, half gruffly, half surprised.

"But I do, and I am expecting something to happen to you every day."

"What for, pray?"

"Because you are always asking God to curse you, body and soul; and I am afraid He will take you at your word, for He says of such as you, 'As he loveth cursing, so let it come unto him; as he delighted not in blessing, so let it be far from him.'"

"Lawk, missis, why you don't take account of such talk as that, do you? Why we all talk that ways, but we don't mean no harm by it."

"It doesn't matter about my notice of it; but He who said, 'Thou shalt not take the name of the Lord thy God in vain,' has said also, that 'for every idle word that men speak they must give account in the day of judgment.' How do you think the repetition of your language will sound in your ears then, my friend?"

"Well, it wouldn't be comfortable, certain sure; but it comes out natural like; you wouldn't hear one fellow in fifty as doesn't rap out just the same."

"I know it, Jacob. It is an awful fact that most of you sin in that way almost as often as you speak; but now I want you to be the one in fifty that will set a better example. Let us seek to have God's blessing over yourself, your work, your home, and family, and we shall soon see you another man. The very fact that it comes out, as you say, quite naturally, proves that you want a new heart, to resist and check this nature so full of sin. If you will learn to use the name of the Lord in earnest prayer, you will soon find it impossible to use it in blasphemy and anger. Try, Jacob: ask for the spirit that loves to call God, 'Abba, Father,' and His adopted child will be jealous of uttering or hearing His name except with love and reverence."

"Well, I daresay it would be a deal better; but then, you see, we've most of us got ugly tempers of our own; and when we gets angry out comes ugly words to match."

"So it is, no doubt; but what's the use of the ugly temper? The same power that can keep in the tongue can help you to be rid of the temper too. The grace of God does nothing by halves, and nothing is impossible with Him. Think of this in time, Jacob, before you have a nest of hornets round you in your own dear children, who will sting you with your own sin."

"I reckon they won't, though. Thank ye, ma'am, for coming right out with the truth, for it is the truth; and as sure as my name's Jacob, I'll try your way."

"A namesake of yours once resolved to get a blessing from God, and he never gave in till he got it. You follow his example; and, instead of fearing that some dreadful thing has happened to you and yours, I shall know that all things are working together for good, and that, instead of 'the curse of the Lord in the house of the wicked,' you have the experience of the promise that 'He blesseth the habitation of the just.'"

We did all we could to help the struggle out of sin and habit; and after teaching a sort of ploughman's song to Jacob's little ones, that they might sing it to their father, it so pleased him, that, being at a loss how to converse with his horses when he would no longer swear at them, he used it instead of his former jargon, and might be heard over many a field, chanting by snatches:—

"Onward, Dobbin, straight and slow;
Firm your tread, your work you know.
Tear up weeds, and crush the root,
Prepare the soil for seed and fruit.

You and I will do our part
With ready will and cheerful heart.
Now right about, good fellow, so;
Along and back again we go.

And when springs up the living grain,
'Neath warming sun and cooling rain,
The Lord of harvest grant that here
A plenteous crop may crown the year.

So, onward, Dobbin, cheerly now:
A patient hand doth guide the plough;
And gentle words shall cheer our way,
And rest succeed the toils of day."

CHAPTER II.

The Pedlar

Most towns and villages have their periodical hawkers, who carry on a profitable trade, if an opinion may be formed from the fact of their persevering reappearance; and it required much of my mother's watchful care to save her invalid from their persecution.

However, one day, as I sat quite alone, a man laden with a large basket of earthenware presented himself before me; and without heeding my assurance that we did not require anything of the kind, he deposited his load on the path, and in a few moments surrounded my chair with plates and dishes, jugs and china vases, while with a civil but voluble tongue he poured forth the praises of his goods for cheapness, beauty, and durability.

It was annoying and disagreeable; but I did not forget my dear mother's desire that these intrusive persons should always be treated with kindness, though with firmness also, at her door. She said it was a hard and toilsome life, and subjected those who pursued it to many rude, ungracious words, and many selfish bargainings, which she believed often needlessly roused enmity, and increased the temptation to falsehood and fraud. She inculcated decision in dealing with them, patience with their troublesome perseverance when refused; and she insisted that the time spent in speaking kindly, and closing the door upon them gently, was not lost, but formed a part of the Christian exercises in the ministry of life.

Just as my forbearance was getting severely taxed, my mother suddenly appeared. I knew she would be annoyed at my position; but she did not allow even her affection for me to set aside the exercise of those principles which she had learned from the word of her God, and which, she often said, were more truly developed in the little affairs of daily life, than in the weightier matters that arrest the world's attention. "A conscience void of offence," she would say, "is a most sweet companion, dear Ruth: it is not the ground of peace, but it is one of the handmaids, as it were, attendant on the heart that rests on Jesus; and there is no balancing of duties before Him — no setting off a few little faults against one great virtue, keeping up alternate light and shadow in the conscience. No, we must try to exercise ourselves, as the apostle calls it, in avoiding offence towards God and man."

She advanced quickly towards us, and the man looked abashed for a moment before the calm dignity of "the real mistress."

"Friend," said she, "have you a home, and children?"

"Why, yes, I has, bless 'em; else mayhap I wouldn't be walking my legs off to earn a penny for their bread."

"Then do at once as you would wish done by a daughter of your own on whom

God has laid the hand of affliction. Put up your things and go quietly away."

"Well, I beg pardon. Miss didn't say she was ill; and we gets so many doors shut in our faces, that if we catch sight of a lady to speak for herself, we hopes to do a bit of business. No harm done, I hope, ma'am."

"I hope not, excepting your own useless trouble in unpacking these wares."

"As to that, 'nothing venture, nothing win,' as the saying is. But now isn't there anything your ladyship would buy of a poor fellow, just to lighten his load? You shall have anything here a bargain, dirt-cheap, my lady, and no profit to me, no not a penny. See now—this lot, a real bargain."

"I do not buy bargains, and I do not deal with persons who will not speak the truth."

"The truth, my lady? I'll swear to every word I say."

"Not in my presence," said my mother, gravely. "And you mistake if you think I am to be imposed on by a show of liberality on my behalf. You require a suitable return for your outlay, your labour, and time, and if I do not give it I injure you."

"Why, sure that's the very thing," exclaimed the man, with delight. "If people would remember that, and not higgle and grumble over the price of a thing, wanting it for less than it can be got anywhere else, maybe we shouldn't say so much about bargains."

"But if you demand more than that honest return, you would injure me," added my mother.

"Well, ma'am, it ain't difficult to see who ought to begin to mend first. Ladies what hasn't their living to get shouldn't grudge the honest price to them that has."

"Still, if you cannot reform the buyer, begin with the seller; and try if, in the end, honesty will not prove the best policy."

"Well, my lady, begging your pardon, you can't know my business as well as I know it myself. See if I shouldn't starve on your plan, pretty soon. But it's very good advice, I dare say; and now wouldn't you buy something, if it's only to help me remember it?"

"Practice will be the best remembrancer, and you shall have an opportunity of trying it if you choose. I will give you a list of some articles I shall need by the time you come this way again; and if you bring them sound and good, at a price which injures neither of us, and serves both, I will purchase them."

"I'll do it, then, as cheap and good as any dealer in the land, so I will; but then —" and he hesitated—"you see, my lady, I beg pardon, but you may be out, or engaged, or forget; and then perhaps I'll get the door shut in my face, as it happened to me just now; and it makes a man angry to be served like that, as if his time was worth nothing but to be wasted by his betters."

"I think that will not happen here," replied my mother, "or I should not have spent my time in speaking to you, as one who not only regrets the manner in which you trade, but who wishes to help forward a remedy. I shall ascertain the proper price of the articles I order, and will not purchase at all if I find you either attempting to impose, or pretending to distinguish me by a bargain."

The man promised to appear again that day month.

"If it please God," said my mother, "to whom we are both responsible, and if we regard Him who not only sees actions, but searches hearts, we shall seek no unworthy advantage one over the other."

The hawker kept his appointment, and my mother kept hers, and at some little cost, too; for a friend from some distance had just called, congratulating herself upon having my dear mother's exclusive attention for an hour or two, and who, when she found that a travelling hawker was to be allowed an interview, insisted upon going away before he arrived.

"It is impossible for you to escape in any reasonable time," said she, "when once you become visible to such people as those. One may sometimes obtain a bargain, but it is at the cost of being talked to death, or perhaps of some positive rudeness."

"Do not fear that I shall be detained unnecessarily," said my mother. "I know exactly what I want, and the price I shall give; so there will be no delay."

"Oh! do bid him call some other day," pleaded our visitor; "it will be all the same to him."

"No," said my mother, "it would do him harm; and it would be wrong in me to waste his time, or disappoint his just expectations."

"Then good-bye, for here he comes, laden with goods enough to occupy you all the day. I must come again when you have no such affair on hand."

And our friend hurried away, making it apparent to the hawker that she had been "sacrificed," as she called it, to the punctual observance of the engagement with him.

The selections were made, and the articles were written down on a small slate which my mother held in her hand, the purchase being more extensive than the hawker seemed to have anticipated; and in the joy of his heart, I suppose, he added a little ornamental trifle, saying, "it should go with the rest, if the lady decided to take the whole."

"No, thank you," said my mother. " do not require it, and you cannot afford to make presents to people to whom you owe no particular gratitude for buying what they want. Now, then, the prices of all these things."

I could see that the hawker stole a glance at my mother's calm, firm countenance, which seemed to say, "If you attempt to impose, our treaty must break up;" and after some little hesitation he named his prices.

My mother calculated the whole, and said, "They come to a little more than the sum I should have paid at the china establishment at B——; and it would have cost me the difference in carriage to procure them thence. If you are satisfied, I am so."

"Well, ma'am, I don't grumble; but maybe you'll give me a taste of something after the load I've carried this morning."

"Are you hungry?" asked she, looking up at the round, bluff face of the man.

"Not exactly that, my lady, only thirsty; and I'd like to drink your ladyship's health."

"Your good wishes for my health would have no additional value from that way of presenting them; and I dare not minister to that besetting sin of my countrymen, drinking for pleasure. If you are thirsty, I will order a glass of water for you."

"Well, I'm not so unpolite as to refuse it, if your ladyship thinks it best. You've been an honourable customer; and mayhap I shouldn't be the worse for meeting more of the same sort."

"This little book will say for me much that I might find pleasure in telling you: may I hope you will read it?" and handing the amount of her purchase on a little tract with a pretty cover, my mother withdrew, and sent the servant to remove the ware into the house, and offer the glass of water.

"I'll tell you what," said the man, in a low voice to our Christian servant, "you've got a queer missis. She's an evangelical, or a Methodist, or something of that sort, isn't she?"

"She reads her Bible, and minds what it says, if that's what you mean," said Martha.

"Well, it's a very good sect, whatever it's called; and if I'd got a few buyers as straightforward and honest, mayhap I'd be thinking of following the good example. But now, you see, though I've done a bit of fair dealing here, and the feeling of it is pleasant and comfortable like, I daresay I'll have to be a bit of a rogue at the very next bargain I make."

"Then," said Martha, looking earnestly in his face, "you will be a worse rogue than ever you were in your life, for you have had a good lesson here, and the knowledge of right is uppermost in your mind at this moment. The little book, perhaps, will remind you, if you should forget."

"Will it teach me to sell to profit now, think you?" said he, as he lifted the lightened basket on to his head.

"Yes, it will teach you about the best riches, and the profit of the man who should gain the whole world, and yet lose his own soul;" and, with a kind wish for his true welfare, Martha considerately stepped down to open the gate before him.

CHAPTER III.

"A Time to Speak"

"Earth has no honest calling,
Life no claim,
That may not on love's altar raise,
'Midst prayer and praise,
A holy flame."

"WHAT a high privilege! what a brilliant honour!" I exclaimed, as one beautiful evening we lingered until the deepening blue of the heavens above us had gradually become spangled with innumerable stars, all sparkling with dazzling lustre."

"To shine as the stars for ever and ever?" said my mother. "I was just thinking so."

"Yes, but it is for those 'who turn

many to righteousness:' there will be no starry crown for me, mother," I replied.

"'But we know that, when He shall appear, we shall be like Him, for we shall see Him as He is,'" she whispered, in that soft, loving tone, that many a time soothed away a passing ruffle of discontent. "Will not that be honour enough, my Ruth?"

"Oh, too much for rebels like me! But there will be exquisite delight for those who shall behold, amidst 'the multitude that no man can number,' some whom they led to the Saviour's feet. Their joy will be more like the joy of Jesus Himself, than that of others who sing His praises for only their own salvation."

"It is very probable that many who never knew the extent of their influence, nor witnessed the fruits of their usefulness here, will find hereafter, to their own surprise, that 'a crown of rejoicing' is prepared for them also," said my mother.

"And those who had no opportunities will not be responsible for the absence of the honour," I said. "So I must be thankful and content."

"There are none without opportunities, Ruth. God has many missionaries, and appoints to each the proper sphere of duty. She who preaches Christ by patience under suffering, thankfulness and contentment through privation, a word in season to the visitor or the wayfarer, is as really, though not so manifestly, at work for Christ, as the evangelist to the heathen, who takes ship amidst the prayers and blessings of a Christian congregation. Yes, dear Ruth, she may be a missionary who never moves beyond her cottage door. The outward stimulus, the charm of sympathy, and the pressure of excitement are not there; but the spring and spirit are the same: 'The love of Christ constraineth us.'"

"Dear mother, pray then that my very helplessness may be of use to somebody. I cannot tell you how I feel tempted to mourn over the suspension of all my pleasant duties among the poor and ignorant."

"If you cannot go to them, doubt not

that, if such be God's purpose, some will be sent to you, my daughter. 'A word fitly spoken,' you know, 'is like apples of gold in pictures of silver.' I believe the true meaning of the word translated 'pictures' is, in reality, 'baskets,' which in that connection is a more intelligible figure for value and beauty. You can select your apples, the pure truth of that holy Word which is more precious than gold, and present it in a manner so loving, so winning, so graceful, that, as a 'silver basket,' it may be worthy of, and commend to acceptance, the treasure it bears. Seek then the fit word; and, 'fitly spoken,' it shall not go forth void."

Long I pondered on my sweet comforter's words, resolving to select some golden apples in readiness for any opportunity, and not forgetting the "basket of silver;" for even "golden apples" ought not to be tossed about indiscriminately, lest they share the fate of "pearls before swine." There must be some connection with, some adaptation to, time and circumstances, else the word may not be "fitly spoken."

If any one had asked me who was likely to afford the first opportunity, I should perhaps have perplexed myself in the choice; but when a willing heart is on the watch for God's opportunities, they will prove neither rare nor difficult.

As I sat out of doors as usual the next day, knitting and meditating, our village butcher came briskly up the walk to ask for orders, stopping in the midst of a tune he was whistling, and raising his hat with genuine politeness when he perceived me.

Understanding that my mother was engaged just then, and saying he could wait a few minutes, he turned again with a look of kindness towards me. "I'm very sorry to hear that you aren't likely to be about again this good while, ma'am; but I hope it's a good sign that you are able to be out in the fresh air here."

"Oh yes, perhaps I may be well again some day; but it pleases God that weakness and pain are best for me at present."

"Well, to be sure now, do you really think so, Miss Ruth?" said Mr. Bell, incredulously.

"Yes, really, for 'whom the Lord loveth He chasteneth;' and is not that a blessed reason for affliction? Besides, it is written that 'all things work together for good to them that love Him.'"

"And by all I ever hear tell, you do love Him, Miss Ruth. But I can't help being sorry to see you afflicted, for all that; though, mayhap, you don't believe me, for some people seem to think that we butchers have no feeling because of what we have to do in the way of our trade."

"I do believe you, and thank you for your sympathy too. There is no reason why persons in your trade should be unfeeling; it is a lawful calling, and a needful though not an agreeable one, and may be carried on on Christian principles just as well as any other."

"I like to hear you say that, ma'am"—and Mr. Bell's round rosy face shone with pleasure—"for I see to everything myself, and all my creatures are killed in the easiest, mercifullest way."

"'The merciful man is merciful to his beast.' No doubt you recollect that. I don't think there is any lawful calling in the world that has not a voice to remind us in some way or other of God and heavenly things, and yours has some very precious memorials."

"Mine! Dear me, I never went so far as that, ma'am; maybe you would just hint any of them."

"Well, you know that you and I are sinners, Mr. Bell, and our Bible tells us that, if we are saved from the penalty we have incurred, it can only be by 'the precious blood of Christ, as of a lamb without blemish and without spot;' for 'without shedding of blood is no remission' of sin. From the beginning of the history of our race, after the fall of our first parents, we are taught this in the type of a lamb offered in sacrifice, up to the time when John the Baptist, pointing to Jesus, proclaimed the fact, 'Behold the Lamb of God, which taketh away the sin of the world.'"

"Well, indeed, I can't deny that I might have thought about this; but, sure enough, it's slipped past me."

"Then there is the character of Christ as well as His atonement often, in its Scriptural figure, before your eyes. 'He was oppressed, and He was afflicted, yet He opened not His mouth: He is brought as a lamb to the slaughter, and as a sheep before her shearers is dumb, so He openeth not His mouth.' We are bidden to imitate the meekness and gentleness of Christ, to feed on Christ, to put on Christ; and so in the shed blood, the smitten victim, the food it supplies, the garments it provides, you have God's chosen emblems of holy and instructive things."

"So there is; and yet I don't think, in the whole course of my business up to this very day, such a thought ever came across me before. However, the next lamb we kill will remind me of something more than its number of good joints."

"And may it also speak a word for the poor sometimes, Mr. Bell. Pardon me for reminding you that the Lamb of God died for high and low, rich and poor; and he that hath no money may come and buy of Him without money and without price.

You have a charity shelf in your shop, I dare say."

"Well, I have so; but it might be better filled, Miss Ruth, and perhaps it may from this time forth. I'm not a hard man, though I ought not to blow my own trumpet."

"The Lord takes note of everything done for His sake; and if you can feed on Him by faith as the life and nourishment of your own soul, you will not forget to feed, as far as you can, both the bodies and souls of others."

"I'm sure I'm greatly obliged to you, Miss Ruth, for this nice bit of talk. You see one gets to think that religion has nothing to do with one's business in this world."

"And so it becomes a godless toil, unsanctified by those holy links which should unite it and us to God, and make it honourable."

"Why, you see one just tries to make as much money as one honestly can, and then one looks forward to retire and be comfortable in one's old age; and we think it time enough to begin serving God when we've got nothing else to do."

"A miserable mistake," said my mother,

who then joined us, " to give Him the dregs of a life spent without Him in the world, when He condescends to allow us to glorify Him if we will, even while serving ourselves: 'Diligent in business, fervent in spirit, serving the Lord,' that is the true wisdom of a man who has the promise of the life that now is, and of that which is to come."

"Well, you see, ladies, I've been used to think myself as good a Christian as my neighbours, though I can't say that it seems all right with me either."

"It is very likely you are, Mr. Bell, and a great deal better than many of them, in all that is upright and good among men; but it is not our neighbour, it is Christ whom we are to follow; and 'if any man have not the Spirit of Christ, he is none of His,' whatever all around him may be. Let us trust Him truly, and we shall love Him dearly; and if we love Him we shall strive to keep His commandments and tread in His steps."

"Ah! but I question if it's as easy as it sounds, ma'am," said Mr. Bell. "There's a deal to do with ourselves even to keep temper and tongue in order among the vexations of business; and if one sets up for a special sort of a Christian, one ought to be very particular, you see."

"Very true; but it was the experience of a deeply-tried believer, a special sort of Christian, that he could 'do all things through Christ,' who strengthened him. 'The Lamb as it had been slain, is in heaven, ever living to make intercession for us, ever ready to give grace and strength to help in time of need."

"Well, ma'am, I hope to think more of these things, for the putting off of them is neither wise nor good, I see; and I have to thank Miss Ruth there for bringing them to mind so kindly this morning. Good-day to you, ladies, and may the Lord bless you."

"'Apples of gold in a basket of silver,' evidently," said my mother, with a loving smile. "Who knows but that this man, in the multitude that cannot be numbered, may cause you the coveted joy that is like unto the joy of Jesus, in the day when He makes up His jewels."

CHAPTER IV.

Change of Abode

THERE are changes in village as well as in town life, but we are not so accustomed to them; and after pursuing "the noiseless tenor of our way" for a happy season, we are apt to forget that it is written, "Because they have no changes, therefore they fear not God." It is, therefore, our wisdom as well as our peace to have our hearts "stayed" on the Unchangeable One, that we may not be "afraid of evil tidings;" and it is part of the discipline His children need during their earthly education to learn that "we have no continuing city here." In "the secret place of the Most High," abiding under "the shadow of the Almighty," is the only tranquil refuge where

"The changes that will surely come,
We need not fear to see."

I should have been glad of rain and clouds one lovely day to excuse myself from taking my usual place in the garden-chair; but I knew it was weak and foolish, and I tried to overcome the oppressive feeling. But it was no small trial to see those waggons lumbering past, containing the furniture of the best and most beloved friends we had in the neighbourhood, with whom for years we had taken sweet counsel, and walked in Christian fellowship. How the whole village would miss the manly character and good example of their friend and patron, the thoughtful sympathy of his wife, the active usefulness of their children. But it was their clear duty to go, for other claims called them to a very different locality; and the parting, as trying to them as to us, must be made.

They came, not together, but one or two at a time, during that sad day, to say farewell. My sweet friend Margaret, the eldest daughter, came alone and last.

"Oh, Ruth," said she, "you will think of us on Sunday; no dear pastor to speak to us, no happy school class, no familiar faces round us; but all cold and dreary, without sympathy, or anything like the spiritual privileges to which from childhood we have been accustomed. I feel as if we were being uprooted from our natural place of growth and nourishment."

"'I am the Vine, ye are the branches,'" whispered a well-known voice over our drooping heads; "'ye have not chosen Me, but I have chosen you, and ordained you, that ye should go and bring forth fruit, and that your fruit should remain.'"

There is nothing like God's own word; it commands attention when the richest human eloquence would be disregarded. Margaret understood all our pastor meant to remind her of in those wonderful words; and as he thus skilfully transferred her thoughts from the human instrument to the Hand that held it, her fears were tenderly rebuked, and her heart comforted.

"You know, my child," said he, "that if the work done in your heart be of mere human influence and partial affection, it must come to naught; but if it be of God, as I trust and believe it is, there is a purpose in it beyond even your own salvation. 'I will bless thee, and thou shalt be a blessing,' was the double promise to the father of the faithful; and we are partakers in its fulness. You are going to be as a light in a dark place, and, not being your own, but 'bought with a price,' must be willing to 'glorify God in your body and spirit, which are His.' Shall I venture to prophesy that before a year has passed away you will not wish to quit your new sphere of duty, even to return among us?"

Margaret shook her head incredulously. It was a time of trial to her young, warm heart, and she had yet to learn how her Lord could supply all her need, "open rivers in high places, and fountains in the midst of the valleys."

"What a blessed thing it is that God's love is not a weak, infirm love, that can yield against judgment, and spoil His children for their crying," said my mother. "He does not willingly afflict, and yet in unerring wisdom He is faithful and steady to do it."

"Our friends will not miss more than they

will be missed here," said the pastor. "I for one shall miss them at every turn, and shall be tempted to wonder who is feeding my sheep and lambs, though knowing all the while that the Shepherd and Bishop of souls will feed and cherish them Himself, the more and better for their apparent privation."

We did not know then how great the change would be to our pastor's feelings in the removal of his true Christian friends, but soon learned that the new tenant in the house, the new owner of the pew in church, the new parishioner of certain standing and influence, feared not God nor regarded man, and loved to thwart and hinder those who did. He was not long in manifesting his anti-Christian principles, and became a sore trial to all with whom his excellent predecessor had worked heart and hand for the benefit of the neighbourhood.

Quietly and constantly the grieved pastor commended him to the prayers of a few Christian friends; and the proud infidel would have spurned, had he known, the conspiracy formed against his evil nature.

"It seems mysterious," remarked the pastor to my mother, "that one so truly a help should be taken away from among us, and this hinderer put in his place; but we must wait and be patient.

> "'Blind unbelief is sure to err,
> And scan His work in vain:
> God is His own Interpreter,
> And He will make it plain.'"

"You ventured a prophecy for our dear Margaret," said my mother. "Will it be presumptuous to believe that this man shall presently be brought, through your means, to honour that Gospel which now he blasphemes?"

"Let us pray on, nothing wavering," cried the reassured pastor, with animation. "All things are possible to them that believe."

Time passed; and one Sunday the bold, rude stare of the unbeliever confronted the meek-spirited pastor in church, and the proud head was a little lowered ere the service ended. This occurred several times, and then Mr. Balman came no more. He was seized with illness, and daily the kind pastor inquired at his door. Then came a request that he would walk up and see the patient, who had just desired that he should be sent for.

Scarcely had he entered the room, when Mr. Balman exclaimed in a stern voice, "Sir, you have come to see a very great sinner."

"Then," said the pastor, "I shall have the joy of telling him of a very great Saviour."

From that time opposition ceased, and the lofty spirit was brought low, and led as a little child into the kingdom of heaven. He lived to promote every good before despised, to walk hand in hand with high and low who loved the Lord Jesus Christ, and to bless God that ever his lot had been cast in our humble village. The rejoicing pastor grew brighter and stronger in faith and prayer, and many an earthly thanksgiving mingled with the joy of angels over the sinner that repented.

In the meantime our valued friends had settled in their new home, among the ignorant and neglected population of a distant county. To do any good they had to begin at the foundation of everything, and to seek co-operation among the few who had influence, hitherto unthought of, and therefore untried. It was no easy task to rouse the apathetic, and persuade people that they possessed talents for which they would be called to give account; and every one who visits among the godless poor, knows how difficult it is to kindle interest concerning heavenly things while the wants of the body are the constant and sole subjects of effort and anxiety.

But patient, persevering love does wonders; and within the year suggested by her former pastor, Margaret wrote of his prophecy fulfilled to the very letter. She was surrounded by a class of Sunday-school children; she had found here and there one of God's hidden ones who could respond to the voice of Christian love; she and her mother and sisters had their cottage readings, their meetings for needle-work, their Bible and missionary branches; and their district began to assume a new and promising aspect.

"Surely," wrote she, "our Lord sent us here, and here it is our duty and pleasure to be. We work for Him, under Him, and look only to Him for help and encouragement;

and though we do cherish the tenderest and most grateful remembrance of former privileges and enjoyments, we feel that they were vouchsafed to us for distribution among those less favoured, and that selfish regrets must give place to willing concurrence in our father's plans, which honour us but too highly in permitting us to assist in their execution. Yes, dearest friends, you were right; we would not prefer to be anywhere but where we are, trying our humble best to obey our Lord's injunction, 'Occupy till I come.'"

Doubtless some will as truly rejoice that the Christian family was called away from our village, as the once infidel that they ever came to it; and all will unite to declare that "He led them forth by the right way."

CHAPTER V.

"Bettering Myself"

"FOR shame, James; you'll come to no good if you do so."

"You mind yourself, and don't talk to me," roughly answered the youth spoken to. He was speaking with insolence and contempt to his mother, who was reproving him for conduct which was bringing trouble on himself and his family, when the young man thus warned him in passing. "I'll teach Will Dawson to lecture me, so I will," angrily continued James. "He wants to be a pattern, I suppose."

"Well, he is a pattern, too," said James's mother, with a sigh; "he is the comfort of the house at home, they say."

I did not hear James's answer, for they passed on, but I had heard enough to make me think of the solemn contrast between him who "honours" his parents, and him who regards not that holy command of God.

It was not more than a year or two after, that one of our village maidens, whom I had tried to instruct, looked over our hedge, then blooming with May blossoms. "Miss Ruth," she said, "will you look up when I pass your cottage door next Monday morning?"

"Look up, Ann? Yes, if you let me hear that you are passing: why not?"

"Oh, only because you won't like it—you'd give me a lecture, I dare say—good-bye, Miss Ruth."

"Stop, Ann. What are you going to do? Surely you are not leaving your nice respectable place at Mr. B.'s?"

"And what if I am? I hope you are not against me bettering myself, Miss Ruth? I've a deal to put up with, I can assure you. Service isn't covered with roses, no more than anywhere else, as I can see."

"I am very sorry to hear you talk in this way, Ann: there's something wrong, I fear.

Will you come and see me for half an hour the first time you have a holiday?" I thought Ann looked rather sly and pert, as she answered, "Oh yes, I shall have a holiday soon, and I'll be sure to come; but I'm set upon bettering myself, and you'll soon hear the way I'm going to do it."

I pondered what the silly girl could mean, but I did not hit upon the right thing at all. Ann was scarcely eighteen years of age, one of a large family, and my mother had obtained a situation for her as under-housemaid in a respectable establishment, where we hoped she would rise in the opinion of her employers, and set an example of usefulness and industry to her younger sisters.

"Bettering herself," thought I. "Does she remember the only way to do that, I wonder?" I had taken care that she should at least know in words that the path of "betterness" is in following Him whose footsteps traced the way of life and glory, and who is at once our "wisdom, righteousness, sanctification, and redemption."

Monday morning came—a sweet May morning—and I sat out in our little garden somewhat earlier than usual, feeling peaceful and happy beneath the spring sunshine and my dear mother's bright smile, as she pursued some gardening operations among the flower-beds. Suddenly the sound of many passing footsteps caused me to do as Ann had asked me, to "look up," and truly there she was, glancing towards me with a merry, saucy face, little aware of the surprise, as well as the regret, with which I should now comprehend her mysterious words.

Leaning upon the arm of James Lawless, the wild, reckless, idle village youth, came Ann, dressed in white bonnet and ribbons, a new gown and mantle, and white gloves. Behind came several young couples, all displaying something white in their dress, and laughing, chattering, dancing along, followed by a straggling train of village children. Ann nodded to me; and my mother, who was just then weeding under the hedge, unseen, heard her say, "There, James, that's the old woman that would have lectured us both, if she'd known what we were after to-day."

"Children," said my mother, raising her stately figure till her head was visible above the hedge, to the instant confusion of the giddy bride, "if you had taken counsel at the word of the Lord, you needed not to fear an old woman's lecture."

"Why, mistress, what is it? Aren't you glad to see young people a bettering theirselves?" said the young husband, pertly.

"God grant it may be 'for better,' and not 'for worse,'" said my mother. "Oh, seek God's blessing, young people, and begin the world with Him, else sorrow will surely come of this day's hasty work."

"Well, we shan't ask your help out of it, any ways," said James, "so you can keep your sermons for them as wants 'em;" and in a moment more husband and wife, over whose youthful heads the Divine blessing had just been invoked, were out of sight.

"Bettering herself," said my mother, sadly, as she came up the walk. "Poor foolish girl! how little is she prepared for the duties and self-denial of a wife, and the management of a home of her own."

Poor Ann! her self-importance and her holiday time did not last very long ; and she who that morning walked first in the bridal train, exulting in being married before so many of her young acquaintances, was soon scarcely to be seen in decent clothing, or ever with a smile upon her once bright face.

In the first place, James Lawless had no home to which to take a wife, and his mother, in desperate indignation at his daring to think of burdening her with a daughter-in-law, refused to allow them to stay in her cottage unless they paid like "proper lodgers;" and as for "doing for him" any more, he must look to his fine-dressed wife to cook and sew, and make him comfortable the best way she could.

Now Ann had no notion of being "put upon" by a mother-in-law to whom she had done the great favour of marrying her bad son, one whom everybody had long said would come to "no good;" for James was a disobedient son, and what disobedient son ever made a good husband? He was idle and selfish, and what idle, selfish youth ever made an industrious, trustworthy workman? True that the grace of God could cause such blessed changes; but James had neither love nor fear towards God, and so it was not likely he would come to much good either in his domestic or public life.

Ann had thought of nothing but that James Lawless admired and flattered her exceedingly; and he offered her marriage just when she happened to discover that Willy Dawson, the steady young gardener at Squire B.'s, had bestowed his honest heart elsewhere, whence she had presumed to boast that she could detach it, and failed in the base attempt. And so, after expending her wages on wedding finery, and giving up her promising prospects as a smart young servant, she passed off the scene of single life into the cheerless gloom of a poor miserable home, and the more miserable condition of a disappointed, grumbling, neglected wife.

Grumbling soon became scolding; idleness brought sulkiness and slovenliness, and James began to visit upon his trying and disagreeable wife the consequences of his own faults, which continually hindered him from constant employment. He thought himself quite justified in preferring any society to hers, and when intoxicated resented her reproaches, and descended to the cowardice and indignity of blows. Oh, what a melancholy picture did the wretched girl present as, still only a little more than twenty years of age, she ran with her infant in her arms, and a little screaming creature just able to hold on by her ragged gown, to take refuge in the house of her parents from the drunken cruelty of her husband!

Ann's mother looked half angrily, half pitifully on the plight of her child. Ah! had she done all she might to have hindered such a state of things, by restraining folly and self-will in earlier days? Had she not too easily given in to the notion of premature settlement in life? and had she not failed in due guidance concerning the character and prospects of the man to be accepted as a husband? Surely, surely mothers have as sacred a duty to fulfil in this as in any event of a daughter's life.

Ann's young sister, much what Ann herself had been two years before, and then at home, stood listening to the tale of the poor wife's wrongs, and the cries of the little children, until she suddenly exclaimed, with a burst more of contempt than of compassion, "Lawk-a-daisy, Ann! and this is the way you 'bettered' yourself, to be sure!"

"Oh, Liddy, don't ever marry!" sobbed Ann. "Men are the wickedest creatures on earth."

"It isn't the marrying, silly one; nor it isn't the men altogether; it's the wrong time and the bad choosing that's at the bottom of such trouble as yours."

So commented a sensible neighbour who had followed the young woman, in fear that she had really sustained some serious bodily harm from her husband's violence, and who afterwards came to tell us what had happened.

And what was Ann Lawless to do now? Oh, first she would go before a magistrate, and get her husband "bound over to keep the peace," and she would starve and die before she would ever live with him again.

But the children, poor little helpless, dirty, frightened objects, what was to be done with them?—the workhouse? Their father was an able-bodied man: would the parish be burdened with his neglected children? Surely she must work. Not among the cheerful group in the servants' hall at Squire B.'s, well fed and well clothed, well warmed and sheltered, without a care at her heart or a cloud on her brow; but as washerwoman, charwoman, weeder, potato-picker—anything by which she might earn a shilling or fifteenpence a day, to keep herself and her babes from starvation.

James, in the meantime, did not wait for a summons before the magistrate: his wife, he said, had "run away from him," and taken the children with her, and now nobody could blame him for taking care of himself. So he disappeared altogether; and where he went, or what he did, remained unknown to his native village.

Poor Ann! her story is but a too common one both in town and country. Oh, that she, and such as she, may in their day of trouble, even though "reaping as they have sown," turn to Him who alone can bring good out of evil, and seek the only means, through God's mercy, by which character and condition can be really and lastingly "bettered."

CHAPTER VI.

The Mother's Pride

AMONG the attractions which used to induce me to look up from my work or book, as I sat at our cottage door, was that of the troop of village children passing and repassing between home and school. I became familiar with the young faces, and sometimes invited them up the path to exchange a few words of kindness. It was cause for thankfulness to see so many of the future men and women of the neighbourhood under good instruction, and I watched their growth in knowledge and in stature with delight. Among them was a fair bright girl in whom I felt great interest; not so much because she was beautiful, as because I saw she was in danger from vanity, and pride, and flattery; and so I set myself to infuse thoughts and principles which should do battle with these giants, and guard my young friend from their snares.

She who should have done this was weak and ignorant, and so delighted in the external beauty of her child, that she decked her in better clothing than she could really afford, or than suited the station in which she was born. "Everybody says our Milly will be a real lady, and the making of us all," said the foolish mother; and Milly's fair head was filled brimful of nonsense by all around her.

My mother used to talk wisely and lovingly to her when she would come and sit with us for a while, and tried to win her to usefulness and a right understanding of the enduring and better loveliness of character; but Milly heeded not. In time I missed her from the school group, and her smile and nod no longer kept up my hope of doing her good. Then I heard of her at fairs and village dances, giddy and self-sufficient; and all I could do was to pray for her and send messages and notes of remembrance.

One day she stood before me, gaily dressed and in high spirits. "I am going to be lady's-maid at S—— Hall," she said, "and am come to say good-bye;" "and to show off my finery," said every movement also.

"And is God's blessing going with you, dear Milly?"

Milly coloured. "Mother has got me the situation, and I expect it's all right," she murmured.

I made her accept the little Testament that lay in my basket, and she put it in her pocket, hastening away. "I shall often think of you," she said, "so dull as you must be here, miss—no pleasure in life."

"Much pleasure in life, dear Milly, and treasure laid up in heaven: when you think of me, think of that."

Then Milly went with her new friends to London, and her family talked largely of her happiness, her gay doings, and fine prospects.

Another year, and all was over. Milly, disgraced, dismissed, miserable, was supposed to be on her way home. But home was closed against her. The pride of the family, the flower of the flock, should never darken that door again. The father was stern, the mother crushed. Sisters were forbidden to mention her name. The villagers looked and nodded at one another, and said they "knew how it would be;" but while they warned their daughters of Milly's fate, they forgot to check what had led to it; and "braiding the hair, and putting on of apparel," still took precedence of "the meek and quiet spirit, which in the sight of God is of great price."

But Milly, instead of coming home, returned to her own ways, and we heard nothing of her until one day a gossip, to whom my mother had said, "Tell us nothing about her until we may do her good," came up to me as I sat out in my garden-chair, and whispered, "Now is your time, Miss Ruth. I saw her in the Blue Bells bar: she doesn't know I did, but you'll find her there."

I was stronger now, and putting on my bonnet and shawl, went off at once, after telling the errand to my mother. The Blue

Bells was a small public-house at the outskirt of the village. To reach it I must pass the church, and the nearest way was across the churchyard, when the gates were open. They were so now, for a funeral procession had just gone in, and I was hastening across with a beating heart, for I knew whose body was to be committed to the grave that day. It was that of Milly's broken-hearted mother, who had grieved, and drooped, and died; and I doubted not that Milly had at last been found, and summoned to see her, but too late. As I was about to pass through the farther gate into the lane, I saw a female figure crouching among the graves beneath the wall. My heart told me it was Milly, but my sight would scarcely have done so.

Oh, that I could show to every thoughtless young creature, vain of her person, and delighting in finery and admiration, that wreck of my beautiful Milly. It might have driven one back from the brink of that ruin into which she had thrown herself headlong. Gaunt, wreckless, desperate; eyes that seemed to burn in their sockets, staring and tearless;

a voice that seemed to come from some sepulchre rather than a woman's lips. She knew and addressed me.

"They said I should find her here, so I came," she said. Just then the coffin, followed by its mourning train of husband and sons and daughters, was borne from the church to an open grave. Milly sprang up, looked at them and at me, and with a groan of horror fell senseless at my feet. What a meeting for a sinful child, who, eighteen months before, had felt on her cheek the warm kiss of that too-indulgent mother!

Through fever, delirium, and to the gates of death, we watched by Milly in our home. Her soul, oh, it was precious in our sight, and we yearned over it as only those can who know something of salvation.

"Ah! if I had heeded you," she said, "I should not be now the most wretched creature upon earth."

"Hush, poor child!" I said, "you will heed now; and while life is spared there is hope for the wretched."

"Hope! what hope? Can you give me

back my mother? Can you blot out my sin that killed her?"

"The blood of Jesus Christ can do even that, Milly."

"Given up by those who once loved me, scorned by those I once looked down upon, how could your holy God help or pity such a thing as I am? Don't talk of it; I'm too bad, too lost."

"The Son of God came to seek and to save the lost. Do you reject His pity? Oh, Milly, you said if you had heeded long ago, you would have been spared this misery, and now I speak again in your ear God's words of hope and peace. Is not that proof of love, and pity, and forbearance? But it may be, that if you refuse to heed me now, you will be constrained to repeat that self-reproaching lamentation where no voice can meet it with a Saviour's offered help."

"Ruth, Ruth, it's the punishment I feel, it isn't the sin. I wish I had died long ago."

"In your sins, poor child? Then you would indeed have been lost. Rather thank

God for the mercy that gives time for repentance and salvation."

"Dear Ruth, how kind you are! Why don't you spurn me, the poor lost one?" and the voice melted away in tears.

"I love to speak to you as my Bible teaches me, Milly. I read, 'O Israel, thou hast destroyed thyself; but in Me is thine help.' I know there are none upon earth beyond the reach of Him who said He could save to the uttermost all that come unto God by Him."

"But I don't love Him; I have never thought about Him but with terror. What shall I do?"

"Just believe Him, Milly. Dare you rather believe that God, the holy God, whose name is Love, would deceive poor sinners?"

"Oh no, I am not such a blasphemer as to say that."

"Then, dear Milly, listen. You have tried to drive away Jesus, barred Him out from a cold hard heart; and yet still He waits to forgive you, to receive you into His everlasting love, and provide you a home among the holy and the blest. But to do this, He suffered sorrow and death that sinners might be saved. Does He not deserve to be believed?"

"Oh yes, He does indeed. Oh, if I could believe it was for me!"

"It is declared, 'Whosoever will, let him come.' It is for 'sinners,' 'sick' ones, 'heavy-laden' ones, 'weary' ones, 'lost' ones; are you not all these, Milly?"

"I am, I am. Oh, how heavy-laden with guilt! how lost! how weary!"

"Then believe you are one on whom His pitying eye is fixed, and you cannot do so without feeling within your heart that spring of love and thankfulness that will make sin hateful and put true repentance in its right place. 'God commendeth His love toward us, in that, while we were yet sinners, Christ died for us.' To cast our helpless souls on this, is faith unto salvation, holiness, and peace."

Oh, what a blessed privilege to have such

words of winning love wherewith, by the applying power of the Holy Ghost, to meet the uttermost need of those who begin to struggle in Satan's grasp! Those words shall never "go forth void;" they shall be the "sword" to cut the bonds of sin, the fire that melts the ice of unbelief, the medicine to heal the wounds of sorrow. Poor Milly's cold hard heart broke down at last, and the "balm," and the good "Physician" touched the disease to heal and bless.

But this world, with all its domestic pleasures, its opportunities to serve and honour God, its beautiful records of self-denying love, its conflicts and its triumph, its hoary head as a crown of glory, were not for this poor brand just "plucked out of the fire." Her earthly hopes must set in humiliation, remorse, and sorrow; and, after angels had rejoiced over the sinner that repenteth, and the forgiving kiss of her earthly father had comforted the dying hour, we laid her by her mother's side. She had no epitaph as an example to encourage her sex: she was a solemn warning at the entrance of a path that leads to destruction.

Milly was a fair village maiden when she used to pass my cottage door, and little thought, when she decked herself in gay attire, how soon it would be exchanged for the last covering of the grave. But those who "sow the wind shall reap the whirlwind." As Milly's poor mother sowed in her child's heart, so she reaped in her conduct. But Milly herself knew right from wrong, and we must each take our portion of the consequences of choosing evil and rejecting good.

CHAPTER VII.

"Only in the Lord"

"It isn't the marrying, it isn't the men altogether; it's the wrong time and the bad choosing." That was a very wise saying of poor Ann Lawless's neighbour.

Far be it from me to denounce the union of attached hearts in any sphere of life. when it can be honestly said before God and man that no "just impediment" exists thereto. But how many a youth forgets that home needs something more than a pretty face to cheer it, and a deeper feeling than a flirtish admission of his flattering attention in the heart of the woman he asks to share it! And how many a young woman forgets, when she professes to pledge both heart and hand, that life hath cares and duties from which a good wife has no escape, neither should she wish to have!

While my dear mother and I had often sad occasion to deplore the wretchedness brought among the poor by ill-assorted and ill-timed marriages, and knew that many a tax upon the parish, many a charge before the magistrate, many a fearful scene of domestic sorrow would have been avoided by the exercise of the merest caution and common sense in this respect, we were able to prove, that when an honourable opportunity occurred, we had sympathy and pleasure in a bridal morning, and rejoiced in the reward of faithful and consistent love.

Our neat, respectable servant had lived with us from the age of sixteen. She was about nine-and-twenty, when, one evening, as she wheeled my garden-chair under a favourite tree, whence I could gaze on the setting sun, she lingered over some kind arrangement for my comfort, and as I thanked her, she softly said, "May I speak to you a little while, Miss Ruth?"

"Yes, Martha; I have noticed all day that something is upon your mind, and you know you may reckon on my interest in anything that concerns you."

"Yes, dear Miss Ruth, I do know it; and if it wasn't that I can stay any time you please, until you are suited, I shouldn't know how to say what I have to say. But the time has come that I am obliged to speak, for Will Dawson doesn't like waiting much longer, now that his sister is married, and his brother gone to sea, and his mother so nicely provided for, and his own work pretty sure. You know Will Dawson, don't you, Miss Ruth?"

"I am glad to say I do know him, Martha, as a good son, a kind brother, and an honest, industrious man, who may reasonably be expected to make his wife a happy woman."

"I hope so, Miss Ruth," said Martha, with a beautiful light over her pleasant face at this unexpected tribute to her well-placed affection. "We've kept company now going seven years, and he says my name ought to be Rachel. But when first he asked me if I would wait for him, he told me plainly all about his family, and what he wanted to do for his widowed mother and the children, before ever he should think of settling for himself."

"That was wise and right, Martha, and you thought so."

"Yes, indeed, miss; and he said, 'I shall never ask you to go home to them all. My wife shall have a home of her own, tidy and nice; and when she gives up service for my sake, it shall be, God helping me, because I can keep it for her, without her needing to do aught but what a working man's wife may do, without shame to him or burden to herself.' And now he is head-gardener he can afford to allow his dear old mother enough to live upon with her married daughter, who has long wished to share the care of her; and he wants me to see a pretty little cottage he would like to take. So if you can spare me for an hour this evening, Miss Ruth, I am to meet him there."

"Go, and God bless you, Martha, if all is right, and as you say."

"Miss Ruth," said Martha, earnestly, "if I thought he could tell me a lie, I'd break with him this hour, though it broke my heart too. You taught me to love my Saviour first and best, and if Willy hadn't loved Him too, he'd be no husband for me."

"Only in the Lord," I said to myself, as Martha tripped away, having been bidden to bring Will Dawson back with her, that we might learn how best to facilitate their plans, and when to be provided against our own impending loss. Yes, we did know something of this young man, and how much he was respected and trusted by his master's family. We had long suspected, too, that he had a special regard for Martha, though he had never in any way intruded upon our house; and their chief opportunities of meeting must have been at his own mother's cottage, whither Martha had often been sent with little comforts during her frequent attacks of illness.

Martha had a kind and gentle manner, and there was a modest propriety about her style of dress by which she would be known as a respectable servant, understanding her own position, and never apeing the appearance of her superiors. See never seemed to be seeking notice or admiration, but gave her mind to whatever she was doing, as if she meant to do her best with it. She had been a most kind assistant to my mother, and a tender nurse to me during my long and weary illness; and now, after thirteen years of faithful service, we must part with her. How could we help regretting our loss? And yet, knowing what we knew of her, and of her intended husband, how could we do other than rejoice in their prospect of domestic happiness?

Martha was now an orphan, but for the first few years of service she had regularly sent a portion of her wages to her aged father; and the habit of economy she had acquired in order to do so, had enabled her to save something after his death had withdrawn this claim, so that she was not a portionless bride, even so far as money was concerned.

But Martha was a little fortune herself to an honest working man, not in face merely, though cheerful piety and good temper ever adorned it with the most enduring beauty, but in what she was, and what she could and would do. She could cook plain wholesome food in the best and most economical manner; she could sew and mend neatly, and always made her own clothes—not to look as if they were hung upon her in a scrambling hurry, but as if they were intended to fit a neat figure, and suit a Christian household. And in time of sickness no tenderer hand or readier skill need smooth the weary pillow, or prepare the delicacy to tempt capricious appetite. Is it right for any one to undertake the care of house and home ignorant of such things as these, simple as they sound?

"Oh," it may be said—nay, it is said, "such things may soon be learned if needful; and what cannot woman's ingenuity acquire, if woman's love dictate the duty?" Granted, in a certain degree; but better not have them to learn when needed; better let knowledge be acquired, and let love apply it with promptitude and care when need arises. The knowledge ready, self-possession is less disturbed when large demands fall upon the affection called to witness and minister to suffering.

My mother resolved that Martha's faithful service should be worthily commemorated, and presented her with a suitable supply of house linen, and many useful articles of furniture; while I had the pleasure of giving the wedding dress, and some little adornments for the pretty cottage. And what with Will Dawson's relations, and Martha's two sisters and brother, we had a tolerable party to entertain at the wedding breakfast. And our kind pastor came and gave them a handsome Bible, and spoke words of heart-cheer for their outset in a new scene of life, under the protection and blessing of Him who said, "Them that honour Me I will honour, and they that despise Me shall be lightly esteemed."

We could not easily supply Martha's place, but she neither forgot nor neglected us; and the least idea that sickness or sorrow might be threatening us, would bring her first to offer help, or silently perform any office of kindness her affectionate heart and observant eye might dictate.

I wish every young working man would choose as well and wisely as Will Dawson, and that every young woman would wait and test the principles of the man she is willing to accept as a husband.

I believe that Martha owed much to the excellent instructions and training she received from her wise and practical mistress; but while I know that there are many mistresses able and willing to teach and train like my mother, I do also know that among the many heady, high-minded young servants of the present day, there are far more "wise in their own conceits" than those willing to profit by such advantages.

Marriages like that of William and Martha justly strengthen the attractions of domestic life; and if in the providence of God reverses do afterwards come, there is no thorn of self-reproach to increase their hardship, neither will there be lack of friends to sympathise and help.

We often called to see our dear former servant, and rejoiced in her happiness; and her children were the frequent playthings and pets of my mother's leisure hour. We knew that Martha would bring them up "in the nurture and admonition of the Lord," and it was always a sweet privilege to help in her labour of love as opportunity occurred.

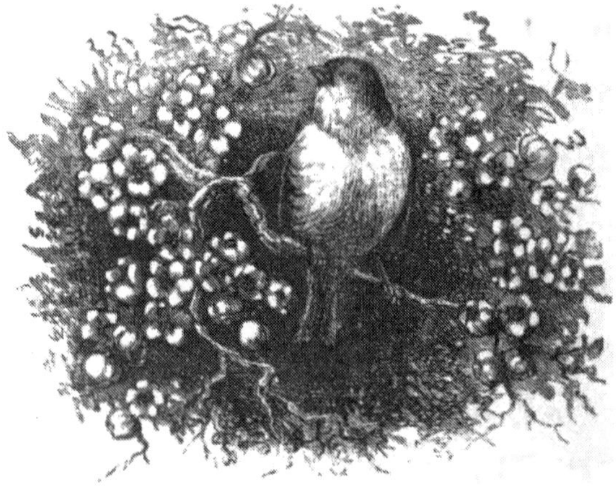

CHAPTER VIII.

The Fashionable Bonnet

"WHATEVER are you doing, Nancy?" asked Bessy Field, popping her head into a cottage opposite to that in which I was sitting, where a young woman sat at the table with a bonnet and ribbons before her, while with her foot she gently kept the cradle, with a fat baby in it, in constant motion.

"Trimming my bonnet," said Nancy. "Missis gave me leave to run home and see what I could do with it while mother went an errand."

"Why, that bonnet isn't worth trimming any more," said Bessy, coming in and taking a seat opposite to her friend.

"What, not this good straw? Why, it's a

real good one, that I bought because it would last. What's the matter with it, pray?"

"Oh, it's so old-fashioned. Why, it's been your best bonnet I don't know how long."

"I do," replied Nancy, quietly. "And it's likely to be my best bonnet a good while longer yet."

"Well, it's too old-fashioned; you should get it made over again."

"I'll make it look fashionable enough, you'll see. Why it goes into every fashion that turns up. I used to set it on the back of my head; then I brought it right over my nose, because, you know, fashion goes by opposites; so I know what I'll do next. It'll have to spread out as wide as mother's best goose's wings when the creature's angry; first backwards, then forwards, so it's sideways turn next; and I bend, and cut, and patch on accordingly. Who says I'm not in the fashion as well as my betters?" And Nancy laughed merrily.

"It's a queer way of doing it," said Bessy, scornfully; "and no one would think it fashionable but yourself."

"Can't help that," said Nancy, quietly, and turning the bonnet round to see the effect. "It's no use minding what other folks think. If I feel comfortable in it, and know I haven't wasted my money for looks, what's the odds to any one else?"

"Well, I don't think you'd like to walk in it to church with me in my new bonnet and flowers," said Bessy, exultingly.

"May be not, if your little brother in his patched jacket and old shoes goes along side of you too, or if the doctor's bill that bothers your poor mother's mind isn't paid yet."

"Nancy, how dare you speak so!" cried Bessy, with flashing eyes and burning cheek. "Haven't I a right to spend my earnings as I choose?"

"No, I can't think it, except you choose to do right with them; and I know what anybody must think of your finery, Bessy."

"I thought just now you didn't care what people think," retorted Bessy, angrily.

"No, I don't, if it isn't true; but if it's true we ought to mind. The Bible says it's what's false that we needn't trouble about; and that's good sense, to my thinking."

"Perhaps you got the notion of your old bonnet out of the Bible you talk so much about," said Bessy, rather scornfully.

"Just so," said Nancy. "It says, Labour with your hands the thing that is good, that you may have to give to him that needeth; and 'Provide things honest in the sight of all men.' Now if I have changes of bonnets as often as the fashion changes, and let my little brothers and sisters go ragged while I go fine myself, I'm not doing my duty; and it's as good to me as if St. Paul or St. Peter wrote me, saying, 'Nancy, don't have a new bonnet yet.' No, no, Bessy; flowers and flounces, and such-like, aren't half as pretty and respectable for you and me as our honest linsey petticoats and neat print gowns. 'Let women adorn themselves with modest apparel,' the Bible says; and whatever you think of my bonnet, you'll not find holes in my stockings, nor slip-shod heels, nor dress that don't become my station. That's what I call modest, and good for the character."

"Well, you're a good hand at praising yourself, Nancy."

"Am I? Then I'm sorry for it, because I don't want to do that, but only to make out what's right, and set it against what's wrong in the thing we're talking about. There's plenty wrong about me, I know," said Nancy, humbly.

"Come now, I'd like to know what you think wrong in yourself, Miss Nancy," exclaimed Bessy, laughing.

"Indeed, I'm not against telling you something that is, Bessy, for it lies on my conscience, and you can help me a little in it, if you will."

"I help you!—a load on your conscience. Well, you are a queer one, however."

"Yes, I suppose I am. It's just this: there's an ornament I want very much, and it's very hard for the like of me to get it."

"Oh, oh! Then this is the upshot of old bonnets and print gowns," cried Bessy, in delight—"you, that want to be so much better than your neighbours."

"Yes, if my neighbours are no better than

me," said Nancy, with a little sigh. "It's 'the ornament of a meek and quiet spirit' that I want. The Bible says it's 'of great price,' and I know there's nothing we servants are more in need of."

"Do you mean that we are to be trampled down, and put upon, just as anybody chooses to treat us?" exclaimed Bessy, in surprise and indignation.

"No, not that. My missis won't trample on anybody, and she's trying for the ornament just as much as me, and says she wants it just the same. But the thing is this. I've got a shocking bad temper when I'm vexed at anything, and Mrs. Marks, you know, who comes to help at our house, did behave badly to me, and I stormed and told her I wouldn't be put upon by her; and Mrs. Marks, she stormed too, and we made such a noise that missis came to us. Well, I was ashamed enough by that time, for all at once it came into my mind that the Lord Jesus was put upon, and spit upon, too, and even struck; and you know nobody dares go as far as that to you and me, Bessy. And then I'd have let Mrs. Marks walk over me, I was so sorry; but I let her go home without telling her so, and I just want you to call and tell her that I'm only waiting to see her to ask her pardon. But one of us might be dead before she comes next time, and missis can't spare me to go so far at present. You pass her door so often: will you, Bessy?"

"Well, I don't know, because perhaps she deserved all you said to her. Maybe it did her good, for she's a cross old thing."

"Oh no! that's not the way to do good," said Nancy, eagerly. "The Bible says we're to 'overcome evil with good,' and not give back railing for railing."

"But what are we to do when we're found fault with for nothing?" asked Bessy, angrily.

"That ain't often, I believe. But if it does happen it's all put down, and they're words that ought to be taught with A B C to everybody: 'What glory is it, if, when ye be buffeted for your faults, ye shall take it patiently? but if, when ye do well, and suffer for it, ye take it patiently, this is acceptable with God. For even hereunto were ye called: because Christ also suffered for us, leaving us an example, that ye should follow His steps.' "

"Well, to be sure, if ever I heard such a thing! Why, we ought to be angels out and out."

"We'd better try after it, Bessy. The Lord wouldn't set us anything to do that couldn't be done, by the help of His Spirit."

"But, Nancy, why didn't you tell Mrs. Marks you were sorry, at once?" asked Bessy, suddenly.

"Because I was proud: the same bad spirit that put me in a passion kept me from speaking to her as I ought, and for a bit I felt evil towards her for setting my temper up; just as if she could have done it if the mischief hadn't been in me. Well, now, what do you think of my bonnet?" she added, holding it up to view as she put in the last stitch.

"Why, I think you'd better put it on and go round in it to see Mrs. Marks, and you'll be all of a piece inside and out."

But it was nevertheless a fact that Bessy's respect for both bonnet and wearer had involuntarily increased, though she did not choose to show it.

"Well, I shall the first time I get leave out; but my time's up now: here's mother, so good-evening, Bessy: you and me ain't properly dressed, you know, till we've got the ornament; let us try hard for it."

"You're an ornament yourself, now," cried Bessy, as the young woman quickly tied on the bonnet, fashionable enough in its wearer's eyes, kissed her mother and the baby, and ran smiling away.

Bessy was right; she was a diamond, though at present somewhat unpolished, but a precious "jewel" nevertheless.

Oh, for more Nancys to bless the households of the land! Might not more simple Bible teaching, with reference to position and duty, and its practical bearing on daily life, do something towards such an end?

CHAPTER IX.

The Shepherd and his Bible

THERE were seasons, especially in the long summer evenings, when my mother would take a seat beside me, and tell me stories of her girlhood, which she had chiefly spent in Scotland, with a grandmother. I remember at this time an account she gave me of an old Scottish shepherd, whose name was John Morland. He was a shepherd, not among green pastures and still waters, but among the purple heath-beds of more northern hills, and over as light-heeled and lawless a flock as ever cropped the mountain thyme. His fleecy charge, indeed, knew no law but that which came from the old grey sheep-dog, and obeyed no bidding but his call.

John Morland lived in a lonely nook, high up among the hills, where a stream found its way through a channel, sometimes swept by a foaming torrent of the colour of coffee, at others easily crossed by stepping-stones. For years he watched his sheep, and wandered over his cloud-swept hills, with scarcely a thought beyond the present employment. Like his flock, he woke in the morning to eat, to roam, to ruminate; and at night to return to his humble bed, without the thought that there was a soul within him wholly uncared for, unfed, and unsaved. For the sound of the Sabbath bells had never broken the echoes of those lonely uplands, and few of the scattered inhabitants thought of going so far as to the place of worship, four miles distant. Once in a way, when there was leisure, a shandy might be seen, sallying forth, conveying a farmer and his well-to-do wife to church; but the day never came when the poor shepherd was not wanted to overlook his black-legged flock. Keeper would have been lost in astonishment at such a movement on his master's part; and there is no saying to what far-off pasture the wild creatures would have betaken themselves in the interval. What wonder that Nature's beautiful and deep teachings were unrecognised in the dull soul of this quiet, silent son of the desert? Nature, so eloquent when interpreted by grace, speaks but an unknown tongue to the soul of unregenerate man.

Was there no spot of promise, no hope, no glimmer in that cottage on the moors? Yes; on a high, dusty shelf there rested an equally dusty Bible, and overhead, out of sight, an eye of love was watching; the Chief Shepherd was regarding the wandering shepherd of an earthly flock.

Illness came, and laid him long in a very quiet corner. The peat-smoke—which first spread through his dwelling, then escaped as best it could, by door and window nearly as much as by the lawful passage—was a dull atmosphere to live in after those free, clear, sweeping hill-tops. He found it sad work to listen to the babbling brook day after day, instead of the active calls of duty between dog and master, the scream of the curlew, and the song of the skylark. He could not, somehow, forget, while lying there all alone, that he must die. He was familiar with a rude Celtic burial-place, cromlech-like, on the summit of the neighbouring hill: he had often sat on those rough stones, traced all over with green continents mapped out by the lichen, and had wondered what sort of men had lived in such far-off times. But in these days of sickness he could only think of what they are now, how they died, and where they went after death. Thus the lesson and the inquiry came down, through unknown centuries of past existence, to himself; and the painful, harassing question was ever stirring within him, "What will become of me when I die?" Doubtless the Spirit of God wrought in this. The love is the same, the ways are various, by which "He commandeth all men everywhere to repent."

At last he turned to that Bible on the dusty shelf. He had no preacher, no teacher to point out the scheme of love and mercy unfolded in its pages; so, in very weariness and restlessness of spirit, he "began to read at the beginning;" and he "read on" (so he said) "to the end." Nor was he far wrong in this straightforward plan of reading the Scriptures.

Had he often looked out with a quiet eye on the tender herb of the mountain, and on the heath of the moors, and on the scanty harvest field barely repaying its culture, on the only bit of arable land near by; and had his eyes been made keenly attentive to the motions of the heavenly bodies, by his daily work and nightly watching over his flock? In the beginning of the Scriptures was the story of the creation and ordering of all these; here was God manifest as the Creator.

He read at length of the "shepherds" of Bethlehem "keeping watch over their flocks by night;" and he, too, welcomed the light which even then began to shine in his heart with Gospel clearness. When he came to that page where "the lost sheep" is found, and is borne home on the shoulders rejoicing, he saw his former self imaged forth in that aimless wanderer. He knew the heart of a shepherd, and what that rejoicing means; and then his heart was touched by the heavenly song, and he was taught to believe that likewise over him, the repentant sinner, there was "joy in heaven among the angels of God."

He had heard or read some of these things before, when he was at school, but it was then only as a tale that is told: now it was life to his soul. The whole mystery was solved by the effectual work of the Spirit, by the Word; and the lonely man in his shieling was rich, because he had found Christ, or rather was found of Him. It was not until he had read and re-read that the blessed truth shone forth in all its clearness from the sacred pages. It came like the morning upon the mountains to his soul, first in streaks of light, touching the clouds of doubt and distress, and by degrees lighting up his whole being.

The life which had flowed into his soul was manifest in deeds of gentleness and love; in a calm joy and simple faith; in a delightful discharge of the humble duties of the station wherein he was called, and in peaceful anticipation of that day when the Shepherd and Bishop of souls should appear to call him to the fold above.

Thus was God pleased to honour the reading of His Word, and by its means, and the teaching of the Holy Spirit of promise, alone to make him "wise unto salvation." Is anything too hard for God? He who knew the difficulties, hindrances, and destitution of this solitary shepherd of the hills, overflowed them all by the tide of His grace, and made him a witness to the glorious fulness of the volume of inspiration, making him to testify that it is truly "Christ from beginning to end."

Thus I have related some things which I saw and heard when seated at THE COTTAGE DOOR.

Pardon & Sons, Printers, Paternoster Row, and Wine Office Court, London.

ILLUSTRATED TABLE BOOKS.

8/- each. In cloth, gilt edges.

SEA PICTURES.

Drawn with Pen & Pencil.

By JAMES MACAULAY, M.A., M.D., Editor of the "Leisure Hour," etc.

Mr. RUSKIN says: "This beautiful book is far the best I have ever seen on its subject."

Pictures from the German Fatherland. Drawn with Pen and Pencil. By the Rev. SAMUEL G. GREEN, D.D. With fine Engravings.

French Pictures. Drawn with Pen and Pencil. By the Rev. SAMUEL G. GREEN, D.D. With 150 fine Engravings.

American Pictures. Drawn with Pen and Pencil. By the late Rev. SAMUEL MANNING, LL.D. New Edition. Profusely Illustrated.

Swiss Pictures. Drawn with Pen and Pencil. By the late Rev. SAMUEL MANNING, LL.D.

Indian Pictures. Drawn with Pen and Pencil. By the Rev. WILLIAM URWICK, M.A. Profusely Illustrated with fine Engravings.

Italian Pictures. Drawn with Pen and Pencil. By the late Rev. SAMUEL MANNING, LL.D. New Edition. Revised. Profusely Illustrated.

"Those Holy Fields." Palestine Illustrated by Pen and Pencil. By the late Rev. SAMUEL MANNING, LL.D. With numerous Engravings.

The Land of the Pharaohs. Egypt and Sinai. Illustrated by Pen and Pencil. By Rev. SAMUEL MANNING, LL.D. With fine Engravings.

Pictures from Bible Lands. Drawn with Pen and Pencil. Edited by the Rev. S. G. GREEN, D.D. With fine Engravings.

N.B.—The above three volumes may be had bound together in one handsome book, entitled "THE LANDS OF SCRIPTURE." Price 21s. cloth, gilt edges.

ILLUSTRATED GIFT BOOKS.

A New Edition, 8s. handsome cloth; 25s. morocco elegant.

English Pictures. Drawn with Pen and Pencil. By the late Rev. SAMUEL MANNING, LL.D., and the Rev. S. G. GREEN, D.D. With Coloured Frontispiece and numerous Wood Engravings.

"Many a one who is doomed to begin and end his days within a 'cribbed, cabined, and confined' circle, can roam, guided by such a book, at the will of fancy, through sunny glades, by babbling streams, or over breezy moorlands."—*Times.*

Reduced from] THE NEEDLES. [*"English Pictures."*

The Harvest of a Quiet Eye; or, Leisure Thoughts for Busy Lives. By the Rev. J. R. VERNON, M.A., Rector of St. Audries, Bridgewater. With numerous fine Engravings. New Edition. 6s. 6d. elegantly bound.

"I never saw anything more gracefully or rightly done—more harmoniously pleasant in text and illustration."—Mr. RUSKIN.

By the same Author.

Random Truths in Common Things. Occasional Papers from My Study Chair. With numerous Illustrations by eminent Artists. Imperial 16mo. 7s. bevelled boards, gilt edges.

"It seems even better than 'The Harvest of a Quiet Eye.'"—Mr. RUSKIN.

Ingleside and Wayside Musings. A companion volume to "The Harvest of a Quiet Eye." With numerous fine Engravings. Imperial 8vo. 6s. bevelled cloth boards, gilt edges.

RECENT MISSIONARY BOOKS.

Among the Mongols. By the Rev. JAMES GILMOUR, M.A., of Pekin. With Map and numerous Engravings. 8vo. 6s. cloth boards.

"There has been, if our experience serves us at all, no book quite like this since 'Robinson Crusoe;' and 'Robinson Crusoe' is not better, does not tell a story more directly, or produce more instantaneous and final conviction. No one who begins this book will leave it till the narrative ends, or doubt for an instant, whether he knows Defoe or not, that he has been enchained by something separate and distinct in literature."—*The Spectator.*

The History of Protestant Missions in India from their Commencement, in 1706, to 1882. By the Rev. M. A. SHERRING, M.A. Brought down to date, by the Rev. E. STORROW, formerly of Benares. With four Maps. Crown 8vo. 6s. cloth boards.

Madagascar and its People. Notes of a Four Years' Residence. With a Sketch of Mission Work among the Malagasy. By the Rev. J. SIBREE, jun. Map and Engravings. Crown 8vo. 6s. 6d. cloth boards.

"Mr. Sibree's book will be very useful to those who want a compendious account of this curious island, and will afford pleasant and instructive reading to every one."—*Daily News.*

Reduced from] SHEEP CROSSING THE TOLA. ["*Among the Mongols.*"

Our Eastern Sisters, and their Missionary Helpers. By HARRIET WARNER ELLIS. Crown 8vo. 2s. 6d. cloth boards.

Life in the Southern Isles; or, Scenes and Incidents in the South Pacific and New Guinea. By the Rev. W. WYATT GILL, B.A. With Illustrations. Imperial 16mo. 5s. 6d. cloth boards, gilt edges.

Short Chapters on Buddhism Past and Present. By the Right Rev. J. H. TITCOMB, D.D., First Bishop of Rangoon. Crown 8vo. 3s. cloth.

The Children of India. Written for the Children of England by one of their friends. With Illustrations. Small Quarto. 4s. cloth gilt.

HANDSOME ILLUSTRATED GIFT BOOKS.

The Spanish Reformers; their Memories and Dwelling-places. By JOHN STOUGHTON, D.D., Author of "Footprints of Italian Reformers," etc. With many Illustrations. Quarto. 8s. handsomely bound in bevelled boards, gilt edges.

The tragic story of the Reformers in Spain told in connection with the places where they suffered. The volume is richly illustrated, and forms an attractive gift-book.

Footprints of Italian Reformers. By JOHN STOUGHTON, D.D., Author of "Homes and Haunts of Luther," etc. With fine Illustrations. 8s. cloth boards, gilt edges.

"A most interesting and instructive volume"—*Spectator.*

Past and Present in the East. By the Rev. HARRY JONES, M.A., Prebendary of St. Paul's Cathedral. With fine Engravings by Edward Whymper. 5s. cloth, gilt edges.

Winter Pictures, by Poet and Artist. Profusely Illustrated in the finest style of Wood Engraving. By EDWARD WHYMPER. Quarto. 6s. cloth boards, gilt edges.

The Waldensian Church in the Valleys of Piedmont. By the late LOUISA WILLYAMS. A New and Revised Edition, with a View of the Present State of the Waldensian Church and its Missions in Italy. Edited by Mrs. MATHESON. Finely Illustrated. 5s. cloth, gilt edges.

THE PRISON OF THE INQUISITION, BARCELONA.
[*From Dr. Stoughton's "Spanish Reformers."*

BY-PATHS OF BIBLE KNOWLEDGE.

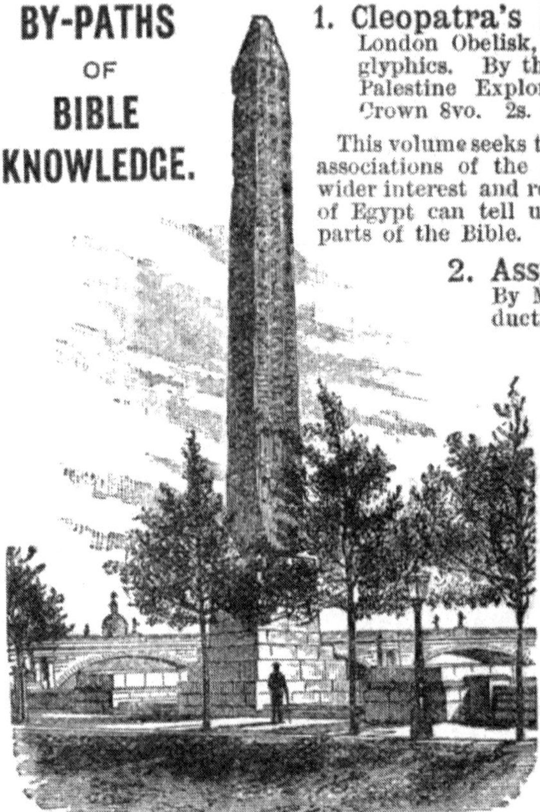

1. Cleopatra's Needle. A History of the London Obelisk, with an Exposition of the Hieroglyphics. By the Rev. J. KING, Lecturer for the Palestine Exploration Fund. With Illustrations. Crown 8vo. 2s. 6d. cloth boards.

This volume seeks to interest the reader in the historical associations of the monument, and also to stimulate wider interest and research into all that the monuments of Egypt can tell us in confirmation of the historical parts of the Bible.

2. Assyrian Life and History. By M. E. HARKNESS. With an Introduction by REGINALD STUART POOLE. Illustrated. Crown 8vo. 2s. 6d. cloth boards.

This little book gives in concise form the latest knowledge of Assyrian history and customs. Very useful for Sunday School teachers and Bible-class students. There is much in it to interest the general reader.

Religions of the Ancient World. By GEORGE RAWLINSON, M.A., Camden Professor of Ancient History, Oxford, and Canon of Canterbury; Author of "The Origin of Nations," "The Five Great Monarchies," etc. Crown 8vo. With Illustrations. 4s. 6d. cloth boards.

Historic Landmarks in the Christian Centuries. By RICHARD HEATH, Author of "Edgar Quinet: His Early Life and Writings," etc. With 84 Illustrations. Quarto. 10s. handsome cloth, gilt edges.

"Calculated at once to give a bird's-eye view of history, and to impress its most important events strongly on the memory."—*Standard*

Sunday Meditations. Adapted to the Course of the Christian Year. By the Rev. DANIEL MOORE, M.A., Chaplain in Ordinary to the Queen, Prebendary of St. Paul's, etc. 5s. cloth boards.

"These meditations are, it is true, arranged for the seasons of the ecclesiastical year, but there is nothing merely sectional about them. They are suitable for all who love the tender and faithful presentation of Scripture truth."—*Christian.*

"There is a wholesome flavour of common sense and catholicity running through the volume."—*Guardian.*

The Authority of Scripture. A Re-statement of the Argument. By the Rev. R. A. REDFORD, M.A., LL.B., Author of "Prophecy: Its Nature and Evidence." Crown 8vo. 5s. cloth boards.

A clear concise statement, in the face of modern objections, of the argument for the authority of Scripture. For the student and general reader.

Christian Ministry to the Young. A Book for Parents, Pastors, and Teachers. By SAMUEL G. GREEN, D.D. Crown 8vo. 2s. cloth boards.

"The author deserves hearty thanks for the freshness, earnestness, and skill which he has brought to bear upon his theme."—*The Christian.*

"We strongly recommend the volume to all ministers of the Gospel."—*Ecclesiastical Gazette.*

ASTARTE.
From "Religions of the Ancient World."

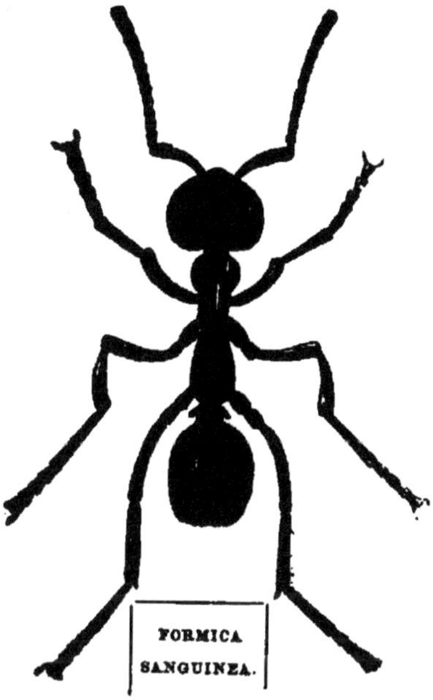

Ants and their Ways. By the Rev. W. FARRAN WHITE, M.A., Vicar of Stonehouse, Gloucestershire. With numerous Illustrations and a Complete List of Genera and Species of the British Ants. 5s. cloth boards.

"As full of interesting information as it is pleasantly written."—*Globe.*

"The author would appear to have given much time to a close personal study of the habits and specific differences of Ants."—*Athenæum.*

"We can safely promise to all who have not read it, that a great treat is in store for them when they do."—*Standard.*

The Chain of Life in Geological Time. A Sketch of the Origin and Succession of Animals and Plants. By J. W. DAWSON, LL.D., F.R.S., F.S.S., etc. With numerous Illustrations. 6s. 6d. cloth boards.

Worthies of Science. Memoirs of Christian Scientific Men. By the Rev. JOHN STOUGHTON, D.D., Author of "Homes and Haunts of Luther," "Our English Bible," etc. Crown 8vo. 4s. cloth boards.

Electricity and its Uses. By JOHN MUNRO, of the Society of Telegraph Engineers and Electricians. With numerous Engravings. Crown 8vo. 3s. 6d. cloth boards.

A popular account of the recent adaptations of electricity—the telegraph, telephone, electric light, electric force, etc. Written so as to be understood without any prior knowledge of electrical science.

The Midnight Sky. Familiar Notes on the Stars and Planets. By EDWIN DUNKIN, F.R.S., of the Royal Observatory, Greenwich. With Thirty-two Star Maps. Imperial 8vo. 7s. 6d. cloth.

"I find in it all the qualities of excellence as a book: lucid, perspicuous at a glance, concise, correct; completely fulfilling its purpose."— *Thomas Carlyle.*

FOR YOUNG PEOPLE.

Twilight Talks; or, Easy Lessons on Things Around us. By AGNES GIBERNE. Illustrations. 1s. 6d. cl.

"The elements of physics simply and pleasingly put; it may be called a dose of physics with the physic taken out of it."—*Rev. C. H. Spurgeon.*

Natural History Scrap-Book. Part I. Animals. Part II. Birds, etc. Fine Illustrations. Oblong imperial 8vo, in coloured cover, 2s. each. Complete in one vol., 4s. cloth boards, gilt edges.

THE TELEPHONE. *From Munro's "Electricity."*

Children's Flowers. The Friends of their Rambles and Play. With fine Floral Illustrations by GIACOMELLI and WHYMPER. Cr. 8vo. 2s. 6d. cl.

A series of pleasantly written and instructive papers on the most familiar wild flowers.

RECENT ILLUSTRATED STORY BOOKS.

Sunflowers. A Story of To-day. By G. C. GEDGE. With four Illustrations. 3s. 6d. cloth boards.

Angel Meadow. A Story of Christian Work amongst the Poor. By the Author of "Field Court." With Illustrations. 2s. 6d.

The Captain's Story; or, Jamaica Sixty Years Since. With an account of the Emancipation. With Illustrations by JOHN GILBERT. Gilt edges, 5s.

Drierstock. A Tale of Mission Work on the American Frontier. Illustrations. 2s.

God's Gifts to Two; or, Margaret Redfern's Discipline. Illustrations. 2s.

Bluebell Talks. Short Instructive Stories in the Language of Flowers, for Young Readers. With Illustrations and Floral Headpieces by E. WHYMPER. Gilt edges, 1s. 6d.

Five Little Birdies. By AGNES GIBERNE. With Illustrations by ROBERT BARNES. In Large Type. For Little Children. Gilt edges, 2s. 6d.

Helon of Alexandria. A Tale of Israel in the Time of the Maccabees. With a Prefatory Note by ADOLPH SAPHIR, D.D. With Illustrations. 1s. 6d.

Hester Lenox; or, Seeking a Life Motto. By HOWE BENNING, Author of "Quiet Corners," etc. With Illustrations. An interesting book for thoughtful Girls. 2s.

Ivy's Armour. A useful and interesting Story for Girls, illustrating Ephesians vi. 13—17. With Illustrations. 2s. 6d.

Luther and Cardinal Albrecht of Mainz. A Historic-Biographical Tale. Given in English by JULIE SUTTER. Portraits. 5s.

Max Victor's Schooldays: The Friends he Made and the Foes he Conquered. By the Author of "My Schoolfellow, Val Bownser," etc. With Illustrations, gilt edges, 3s. 6d.

Straight to the Mark. A Story for Old and Young. By the Rev. T. S. MILLINGTON, M.A., Author of "Boy and Man," etc. With Illustrations. Gilt edges, 5s.

Through the Linn; or, Miss Temple's Wards. By AGNES GIBERNE. With Engravings. Cloth gilt, 3s.

Under Fire: being the Story of a Boy's Battles against Himself and other Enemies. By the Author of "The Boys of Highfield," etc. Illustrated. Gilt edges, 4s.

Recent Biographical Works.

HANNAH MORE.

The Life of Hannah More. A Lady of Two Centuries. By ANNA J. BUCKLAND. With Portraits. Imperial 16mo. 3s. cloth boards.

The Morning Star of the Reformation. The Life and Times of John de Wycliffe. Crown 8vo. 2s. cloth boards.

Vignettes of the Great Revival of the Eighteenth Century. By the Rev. E. PAXTON HOOD, Author of "Isaac Watts: his Life and Writings, his Homes and Friends," etc. Illustrations. Imperial 16mo. 4s. cloth boards, gilt edges.

Isaac Watts: His Life and Writings, Homes and Friends. By the Rev. E. PAXTON HOOD. Illustrated with Portraits and other Engravings. 8vo. 6s. cloth boards.

Memoir of the Rev. Henry Watson Fox, B.A., of Wadham College, Oxford; Missionary to the Telugu people, South India. By the Rev. GEORGE TOWNSHEND FOX, M.A. New Edition, with Illustrations. Crown 8vo. 3s. 6d. cloth boards.

Life of the Rev. Richard Knill, of St. Petersburg. By the late Rev. C. M. BIRRELL. With Review of his Character by the late Rev. JOHN ANGELL JAMES. New and Revised Edition, with Steel Portrait and other Engravings. Crown 8vo. 3s. 6d. cloth boards.

The Life of Jean Frederic Oberlin, Pastor of the Ban de la Roche. By Mrs. JOSEPHINE E. BUTLER. Illustrated. With Map of the Ban de la Roche. 3s. 6d. cloth.

Seventeen Years in the Yoruba Country. Memorials and Portrait of Anna Hinderer, Wife of the Rev. David Hinderer, C.M.S.; Missionary in Western Africa. With an Introduction by Archdeacon Hone. Illustrated. Crown 8vo. 3s. cloth.

Hugh Latimer. A Biography. From original documents. By the late Rev. R. DEMAUS, M.A., Author of "William Tyndale: a Contribution to the History of the English Bible," etc. *New and Revised Edition.* Crown 8vo. 5s. cloth boards.

Religious Topography of England. By S. R. PATTISON. Crown 8vo. 2s. 6d. cloth boards.

An alphabetical list of places with the religious associations of each. A most interesting book, full of fresh and valuable information.

OBERLIN.

ILLUSTRATED STORY BOOKS.

FIVE SHILLINGS EACH.

Without intending it. By GEORGE E. SARGENT, Author of "The Story of a City Arab," etc. With Engravings. Cloth, gilt edges.

The Captain's Story; or, Jamaica Sixty Years Since. With an account of the Emancipation. Cloth, gilt edges.

The Franklins; or, The Story of a Convict. By GEORGE E. SARGENT, Author of "The Story of a City Arab," etc. With Illustrations. Cloth, gilt edges.

A Yacht Voyage Round England. By the late W. H. G. KINGSTON. Illustrations. Cl., gilt edg.

Cobwebs and Cables. By HESBA STRETTON. Illustrated. Cloth, gilt edges.

The Two Voyages; or Midnight and Daylight. By the late W. H. G. KINGSTON. Illustrated.

The Golden Grasshopper: A Tale founded on Events in the Days of Sir Thomas Gresham. By the late WILLIAM H. G. KINGSTON.

FOUR SHILLINGS EACH.

Lost in Egypt. A Story from Life. By Miss M. L. WHATELY. Illustrated. Cloth, gilt edges.

Tales of Three Centuries. The Authorised Translation from the French of Madame GUIZOT DE WITT.

The Chronicles of an Old Manor House. By GEORGE E. SARGENT.

Boy and Man: A Story for Old and Young.

The Foster Brothers of Doone. A Tale of the Irish Rebellion of 1798.

THREE SHILLINGS AND SIXPENCE EACH.

Quiet Corners. By HOWE BENNING. A Book for Young Ladies.

Bede's Charity. By HESBA STRETTON. Cloth, gilt edges.

The Great Salterns. By SARAH DOUDNEY. Cloth, gilt edges.

Philip Gainsford's Profit and Loss. By GEORGE E. SARGENT.

Janet Darney's Story. A Tale of Fisher Life in Chale Bay. By SARAH DOUDNEY. Cloth, gilt edges.

Was I Right? By Mrs. O. F. WALTON, Author of "Little Dot," etc.

A Peep Behind the Scenes. By Mrs. O. F. WALTON, Author of "Christie's Old Organ," etc.

THREE SHILLINGS EACH.

Through the Linn; or, Miss Temple's Wards. By AGNES GIBERNE.

Ermyn, the Child of St. Elvis. By RUTH LYNN. Cloth, gilt edges.

Ethel Graham's Victory. By Mrs. H. B. PAULL. Cloth gilt.

Once upon a Time; or, The Boy's Book of Adventures.

TWO SHILLINGS AND SIXPENCE EACH.

Three Christmas Eves. By the Author of "The Cottage on the Shore," etc. Illustrated. Cloth gilt.

Ivy's Armour. By the Author of "Katie, the Fisherman's Daughter."

Angel Meadow. By the Author of "Field Court." With Illustrations.

Elsie's Footprints; or, Jesus your Life and your Life for Jesus. By Mrs. LUCAS SHADWELL.

The Moth and the Candle; or, Lucy Woodville's Temptation.

Old Anthony's Secret. By SARAH DOUDNEY.

TWO SHILLINGS EACH.

Drierstock. A Tale of Mission Work on the American Frontier.

God's Gifts to Two; or, Margaret Redfern's Discipline.

Paul Harvard's Campaign. Illustrated. Crown 8vo.

Great Voyagers: Their Adventures and Discoveries.

THE GIRL'S OWN BOOKSHELF.

The following volumes of Stories and Miscellaneous Articles taken from the pages of the GIRL'S OWN PAPER are now ready.

Quarto, 6s. handsome cloth gilt.

A Crown of Flowers: Poems and Pictures collected from the pages of the "Girl's Own Paper." Edited by CHARLES PETERS. With Illustrations by M. E. Edwards, Davidson Knowles, Frank Dicksee, A.R.A., R. Catterton Smith, Robert Barnes, Charles Green, John C. Staples, G. H. Edwards, O'Kelly, J. McL. Ralston, William Small, Frank Dadd, and other eminent artists.

Cora; or, Three Years of a Girl's Life. With numerous Illustrations by M. ELLEN EDWARDS. 2s. 6d. cloth boards.

The Girl's Own Cookery Book. By PHYLLIS BROWNE. With Prefatory Note by Sir RISDON BENNETT, M.D., F.R.S. 1s. cloth.

The Queen o' the May. By ANNE BEALE. With numerous Illustrations. 3s. cloth boards.

The Master's Service. A Practical Guide for Girls. By Lady BRABAZON, DORA HOPE, ALICE KING, and MARY SELWOOD. Illustrated. 2s. 6d. cloth boards.

A republication of some of the more popular and useful Papers and Stories which have appeared in the BOY'S OWN PAPER. *Volume I. now ready.*

Adventures of a Three Guinea Watch. By TALBOT BAINES REED. With an Introduction by the Editor of the "Boy's Own Paper." With many Illustrations. Small Quarto. 4s. cloth boards.

RECENT BOOKS FOR BOYS.

The Realm of the Ice-King.—A Book of Arctic Discovery and Adventure. A New and Revised Edition, enlarged, and with numerous Illustrations. 5s. cloth, gilt edges.

Under Fire: Being the Story of a Boy's Battles against Himself and other Enemies. By the Author of "The Boys of Highfield," etc. Illustrated. Imperial 16mo. 4s. cloth boards, gilt edges.

Straight to the Mark. By the Rev. T. S. MILLINGTON, M.A. An interesting Story for old and young, by the popular Author of "Boy and Man," etc. With Illustrations. Imperial 16mo. 5s. bevelled boards, gilt edges.

Max Victor's Schooldays: the Friends he Made and the Foes he Conquered. By the Author of "My Schoolfellow, Val Bownser," etc. With Illustrations. Imperial 16mo. 3s. 6d. bevelled boards, gilt edges. A useful Story for Schoolboys.

Shilling Volumes for the Young.

Each complete in itself, and Illustrated. 1s. cloth boards.

*** *One Hundred and Fifty Volumes have been published. For complete List, see the General Catalogue.*

131. **Mistakes by the Way**; or, Ada's New Home.
132. **Bravely Borne**; or, Archie's Cross. By the Author of "Dick's Strength," etc.
133. **Margie's Gifts and How she Used them.**
134. **A Bit of Holly.** With Illustrations.
135. **Pansy.** A Story for Little Girls.
136. **Next Door Neighbours.** By AGNES GIBERNE.
137. **Minatoo**; or, Little Frankie's Bearer. By Mrs. H. B. PAULL.

123. **Little Strokes Fell Great Oaks.**
124. **Charlie's Log.** A Story of Schoolboy Life.
125. **The Blind Boy of the Island.**
126. **Field Court**; or, Who Maketh Thee to Differ?
127. **Wonders under the Earth.** By JANE BESEMERES.
128. **Adventures of Two Brothers.** By G. E. SARGENT.
129. **My Golden Ship.** By M. E. ROPES.
130. **As Many as Touched Him.** By the Author of "It's all Real True," etc.
138. **Roving Robin.** By NELLIE HELLIS.
139. **Elinor Vincent's Discipline.**
140. **Bernard Kendal's Fortune.** By Mrs. RUTH LAMB.
141. **A Slip at Starting**; or, Johnny's First Place. By EMMA LESLIE.
142. **Some Folk in our Village.**
145. **Selim's Pilgrimage.** A Tale of Hindu Muhammadan Life.
146. **The Mirage of Life.** With Illustrations by JOHN TENNIEL.
147. **Milly's Mistakes, and What she Learned by them.**
148. **Joe Harman's Experiences.**

COLOURED TOY-BOOKS AND CARDS.

Sixpenny Coloured Toy-Books.

The Blackbird's Nest.
Little Antoine and the Bear.
Our Pretty Village.
Rosa, the Little Cousin from India.

Each Book contains Six large full-coloured Pages and Ten Vignettes, with letterpress in large type.

Shilling Packets of Cards.

Morning Rays. Eight handsome quarto Cards, richly printed in Colours.
Light at Eventide. The same Designs, with Evening Texts.
Friendship's Greetings. For Birthdays and other Anniversaries. Eight upright Cards, in Gold and Colours.
Blessings of the King. Richly printed in Gold and Colours.
The Captain of our Salvation. Beautifully Embossed.
Here and Hereafter. Twelve Cards, with Texts.

Sixpenny Packets.

Living Waters for Thirsty Souls. Floral Designs in Gold and Colours.
He is Faithful that Promised. Prayers and Promises. Twelve Cards.
The Pilgrim's Wants. With Verses by CHARLOTTE ELLIOTT, and Texts.
Pearls of Great Price. With Texts.
The Light of the World. Briony Designs, with Texts.
The Shield of Faith. Watchwords for the Christian Soldier.

ILLUSTRATED BOOKS FOR LITTLE PEOPLE.

Five Little Birdies. By AGNES GIBERNE, Author of "Readings with the Little Ones," etc. With Illustrations by Robert Barnes. In Large Type. Quarto. 2s. 6d. cloth boards, gilt edges.

Reduced from "Five Little Birdies."

Katie Brightside, and How she made the Best of Everything. By RUTH LAMB, Author of "Thoughtful Joe," etc. In Large Type, with Illustrations by Robert Barnes. Quarto. 2s. 6d. cloth boards, gilt edges.

Thoughtful Joe, and How he gained his Name. By Mrs. RUTH LAMB. Illustrated by Robert Barnes. In Large Type. 2s. 6d. handsome cloth.

CPSIA information can be obtained
at www.ICGtesting.com
Printed in the USA
BVHW080859191118
533502BV00023B/1394/P